Dd

Ee

Ff

Jj

Kk

Ll

Pp

Qq

Rr

Vv

Zz

ABC Book of Words

Featuring Jim Henson's Sesame Street Muppets

Illustrated by Harry McNaught

dog

Random House/Children's Television Workshop

Library of Congress Cataloging-in-Publication Data:
The Sesame Street ABC book of words. SUMMARY: Busy scenes in which characters from Sesame Street are involved in various activities with different objects introduce vocabulary words and the letters of the alphabet. 1. Vocabulary—Juvenile literature. 2. English language—Alphabet—Juvenile literature. [1. Alphabet. 2. Vocabulary] I. McNaught, Harry, ill. II. Sesame Street (Television program). PE1449.S455 1988 428.1 [E] 86-62405 ISBN: 0-394-88880-4 (trade); 0-394-98880-9 (lib. bdg.)

Manufactured in the United States of America   5 6 7 8 9 0

airplane

Aa

accordion

ants

apples

apple

Bb

beach ball

Big Bird

Barkley

book

Bert

bucket

bathhouse

boat

barbells

bathing suit

butterfly

bottle

basket

bread

banana

blanket

Cc

Cookie Monster

cookies

cow

calf

cowcatcher

Count

Countmobile

cloud

caboose

crane

coconut

camel

car

cats

cactus

canteen

daisies

door

doorknob

dress

drawer

dice

dresser

doughnuts

fly

flower

finger

Ff

flag

eather

fur

fence

foot

Grover

gravy boat

golf clubs

gorilla

glass

globe

golf ball

goose

guitar

game

Garage Sale

Hh

horns

hatchet

hoe

hammer

horse

harness

hose

hat

hand

hook

hay

hayloft

horseshoe

house

Kk

kites

key

light bulb

lamp

ladder

lamppost

Mm

mountain

map

magnifying glass

Mystery of the Missing Mitten

moon

moose

mouse

mitten

noodles

napkin

nest

Oo

onion

oranges

Oscar

orange juice

okra

olive

OLIVE OIL

opener

OATS

owl

oven

Pp

plums

parsnips

peas

peanuts

papayas

peaches

peppers

pears

parsley

potatoes

OPEN

pineapples

pumpkins

plant

Prairie Dawn

pigeons

Qq

quilt

queen

Ss

sprinkler

skate

squirrel

shovel

sandbox

skateboard

stroller

swing

slide

sidewalk

seesaw

soda

sandwich

snake

Tt

television

trombone

trumpet

tambourine

tuba

table

turtle

triangle

tom-tom

U u

umbrella

ukulele

unicycle

violets

vase

valentine

violin

V v

Ww

whale

wave

water

Xx

x-ray

yo-yo

Yy

Zz

zipper

the End

Aa	Bb	Cc
Gg	Hh	Ii
Mm	Nn	Oo
Ss	Tt	Uu
Ww	Xx	Yy